Thrive in the Sharing Economy

Insider Secrets for Making Money with Airbnb, Uber, and More

Table of Contents

Chapter 1. Introduction

Welcome to our Special Report: "Thrive in the Sharing Economy: Insider Secrets for Making Money with Airbnb, Uber, and More". We are living in an extraordinary era of financial opportunity. This untapped resource is right at our fingertips, providing a robust source of income for those bold enough to seize it. From renting out a spare room to offering rides to nearby travelers, the landscape of earning money is transforming dramatically. Our report makes navigating these new territories incredibly straightforward. Whether you're eyeing Airbnb or Uber as your next venture, we have you covered with insider secrets straight from the industry experts. Packed with actionable tips and strategies, this Special Report is your ticket to thriving in the dynamic sharing economy. Get ready to unlock a new world of potential profits, and remember, this is not just about earning—you're set to pioneer this evolution in economy too! How's that for motivation to dive in?

Chapter 2. Understanding the Sharing Economy

Call it the gig economy, peer economy, platform economy, or sharing economy, we are in the throes of a significant shift in how labor, goods, and services are exchanged. At the heart of this shift are platforms that match people who have certain services or assets with those who want access to them. While platforms like Uber, Airbnb, and Upwork are well-recognized names, there are thousands of other platforms driving this new economic model.

Let's begin by trying to understand the core principles underlying the sharing economy.

2.1. The Core Tenets of the Sharing Economy

The sharing economy has its roots in technology-enabled peer-to-peer exchanges. The exchange can be for goods, services or even experiences. This economy propagates the idea of "access over ownership," where individuals or businesses own assets but don't utilize them all the time, and thus, those resources can be shared for profit or sometimes for free. The main elements that underlie the sharing economy are:

- Direct access to goods and services: The sharing economy gives users direct access to goods and services through advanced technology platforms. Everyone becomes both a consumer and producer, redefining traditional roles of buyer and seller.

- Trust: Trusty is an essential ingredient in this equation. Buyers have to trust sellers, and sellers have to trust buyers. Trust is built through various mechanisms, such as profile information, reviews, and other platform features that channel transparency.

- Flexibility: The sharing economy offers unprecedented flexibility in terms of when, where, and how services are being rendered. It gives both parties the freedom to operate as per their convenience.

2.2. The Rise of the Sharing Economy

Although a relatively new phenomenon, the sharing economy has seen astronomical growth since its inception. Technology has been the engine driving this transformation. It has democratized the process, making it easier for anyone with a smartphone to partake in this economic model. The sharing economy has not just brought newer services under its umbrella, but it has also reinvented many traditional business models. For example, in hospitality and transportation, traditional businesses are aligning themselves with the sharing economy by adopting technology solutions and rethinking their operating models.

2.3. Benefits of Participating in the Sharing Economy

For participants – those who are offering their services or assets – there are several benefits that make this economic model attractive. Here are a few:

- Extra income: This is the main attraction for most participants. For instance, individuals rent out their homes on Airbnb for extra income, or they offer rides on Uber.

- Flexibility: Participants can offer their services on their own schedule. This flexibility is particularly appealing to individuals who have other commitments, such as childcare or a traditional job.

- Low barrier to entry: In most cases, the barriers to entry are low. Often, all that's needed is an unused asset (like a car or a room in a house) and a smartphone app.

- Empowerment: Many participants find that taking control of their working hours and income is empowering.

2.4. Understanding the Risks

While there are plenty of advantages to participating in the sharing economy, there are also risks involved. Understanding these risks can help you navigate challenges and make informed decisions:

- Regulatory risk: Often, sharing economy businesses operate in legally gray areas. Uber's legality, for example, has been challenged in various regions globally. Airbnb has faced similar issues in certain cities where traditional hotel industry regulations apply.

- Market saturation: As these platforms become more popular, there is a risk of market saturation, which could limit earning potential.

- Liability issues: Issues such as damage to property or accidents during service delivery can lead to legal and financial liabilities.

2.5. Navigating Regulation

The growth and visibility of the sharing economy have led regulators worldwide to reevaluate existing laws and consider new ones. There is a range of approaches taken, varying from permissive to restrictive. Understanding your local regulations before participating in the sharing economy is critical.

In conclusion, the sharing economy offers a new frontier for earning money and breaking free from traditional work structures. However, like any entrepreneurial venture, it demands an understanding of the landscape, a keen sense of opportunities and risks, and the preparedness to face challenges head-on. As more and more people engage with the sharing economy, it will continue to shape and reshape our socio-economic patterns - an exciting prospect for all forward-thinking pioneers.

Chapter 3. The Art and Science of Airbnb

The sharing economy has transformed travel and hospitality, with pioneer Airbnb swiftly emerging as the driving force. If you own or have access to property, renting it out via Airbnb allows you to turn it into a lucrative endeavor. However, attracting renters and ensuring a positive guest experience is a refined science as much as it is an art.

3.1. Getting Your Property Airbnb Ready

First things first, preparing your property for Airbnb isn't just about cleaning up and handing over keys. It requires careful planning and attention to detail. Make sure your property is deep-cleaned, decluttered and appropriately furnished. Create a tranquil environment, making it as appealing and comfortable as possible. This applies to both the interior and exterior - keep gardens or yards well-maintained.

3.2. Creating a Standout Listing

Your Airbnb listing can make or break your hosting game. High-quality photographs can considerably enhance the appeal of your listing, conveying professionalism and care. Include photographs of every room, ensuring they're well-lit and showcasing all the amenities. Accompany these photographs with clear descriptions, underscoring what makes your property unique.

Craft a compelling title, as this will be the first thing potential guests see. Incorporating pertinent details such as location, views, or unique features will augment its attraction.

Responding to inquiries promptly and maintaining a high response rate will entice guests by putting forth your commitment and empathy.

3.3. The Price is Right

Setting appropriate prices is pivotal in optimizing occupancy and income. Consider location, property size, amenities, and the local competition while fixing your rates.

Harness Airbnb's Smart Pricing feature if required, which automatically adjusts prices based on demand and competition. However, avoid underpricing your property. While this might increase bookings initially, it may devalue your offering in the long run.

3.4. Host Responsibly

As an Airbnb host, you bear responsibilities towards your guests, neighbors, and community. Centering safety, ensuring your property aligns with local regulations, and obtaining necessary insurances are crucial. Strive for transparency in communication, listing all rules clearly and being upfront about any potential drawbacks of your listing.

3.5. Nail The Guest Experience

Remember, you're not just offering a property; you're offering an experience. Go that extra mile to provide local tips, a welcome basket, or personalized touches. Check in with your guests during their stay - but respect their privacy.

A crucial part of the guest experience is a seamless check-in and check-out process. Detailed instructions, with photographs or videos if necessary, will prove helpful for guests and decrease the chance of misunderstandings.

3.6. Manage Your Reviews and Ratings

Reviews and ratings hold immense power in the Airbnb ecosystem. Encourage guests to review their stay and promptly reply to all reviews. Address any issues or criticisms with humility and show your commitment to improvement.

3.7. Hiring a Property Manager

If managing your Airbnb seems overwhelming or you lack the time necessary, hiring a professional property manager is a viable option. They can handle the day-to-day chores, manage bookings, interact with guests, and ensure optimal upkeep.

3.8. Track Your Performance

Keeping a close eye on your Airbnb business's performance is necessary for continuous improvement and growth. Airbnb's Host Dashboard provides a host of metrics such as booking rate, nights booked, revenue, and average daily rate. Use this data to tweak your strategy and boost performance.

Making money with Airbnb is as much a science as it is an art. With this comprehensive guide, you have every tool you need to turn your property into a revenue-generating asset. Start today, and begin reaping the benefits of this thriving sharing economy platform. Remember, host responsibly, prioritize your guests, and your success is inevitable.

Chapter 4. Mastering Uber: Making Every Mile Count

Companies like Uber have revolutionized the way people move around in cities, making it easier and often cheaper than traditional taxi services. However, understanding how to maximize your earnings as an Uber driver requires a strategic approach. In this comprehensive guide, we will explore every aspect of the Uber platform and discuss strategies to maximize your income.

4.1. Understanding the Uber Algorithms

One of the first steps to mastering Uber is understanding the algorithms that power the service. The pricing algorithm hinges on several factors: base fare, cost per minute, cost per mile, and surge pricing. While the base fare, cost per minute, and cost per mile are consistent, surge pricing kicks in during peak demand hours to incentivize more drivers to get on the road.

Understanding these factors and when they apply is key to optimizing your earnings. For example, during off-peak hours, you may find it more lucrative to target longer trips; the cost per mile might earn you more money than the cost per minute.

4.2. Efficiently Scheduled Driving

Knowing when to drive is crucial. Uber traffic and demand differ during the day and week. Generally, weekday mornings (6am-9am) and evenings (5pm-7pm) are considered as 'rush hours'. Weekends, especially Friday and Saturday nights, are also usually busy. However, this can vary by city, so local knowledge plays a significant role.

By aligning your driving schedule with these peak demand periods, you can take advantage of surge pricing and increase the likelihood of back-to-back trips. Yet, remember to take enough breaks to prevent fatigue and maintain your quality of service.

4.3. Selecting the Right Vehicle

Your choice of vehicle can also affect your earnings. More comfortable, newer-model cars might enable you to qualify for the more lucrative UberX, UberSELECT, or UberBLACK services. However, higher-end vehicles also come with higher operating costs, which need to be factored into your calculations.

If you plan on driving full-time, investing in a fuel-efficient vehicle can significantly reduce your expenses and increase your net earnings. This is particularly important if you seek longer trips or drive in a sprawling city where distances might add up quickly.

4.4. Mastering Ratings

Ratings are central to the Uber experience. Not only does a high rating instill greater confidence in passengers, but it also contributes to your reputation as a reliable driver.

Strive to provide the best possible service in every ride. Keep your car clean and smelling pleasant. Be polite, professional, and respectful. An international charger, bottled water, or small amenities like candies can go a long way in improving a rider's experience.

4.5. Navigating Surge Pricing

Understanding surge pricing can greatly enhance your earnings. Surge fees apply when rider demand outpaces driver supply. By strategically operating in areas with high demand or during peak times, you could significantly boost your income.

Uber provides a heat map that shows areas of high rider demand. Monitor this map regularly and position yourself accordingly to benefit from surge pricing. But remember that other drivers will be doing the same, so be prepared for competition.

4.6. Optimizing Route Efficiency

Route efficiency plays a huge role in making the most money as an Uber driver. Waze and Google Maps are two very popular apps that can help optimize your travel paths. The key is to reduce the time you spend reaching a passenger and on the trip itself.

The more trips you complete, the more you can earn. Leveraging these tools can help guide you through traffic jams, suggesting alternative routes to complete your trips faster.

4.7. Taking Advantage of Uber Driver Promotions

Uber often runs promotions that reward drivers with extra money for completing a certain number of trips within a specified timeframe. Keep an eye out for these opportunities. They can provide a quick way to earn extra cash, especially if you're already planning to be on the road during those hours.

4.8. Summing Up

Mastering Uber involves a careful understanding of the platform's algorithms, efficient scheduling, selecting the right vehicle, leveraging surge pricing, maintaining high ratings, optimizing your route efficiency, and taking advantage of promotions. All these factors can significantly improve your earnings, ensuring you make every mile count.

By arming yourself with these tips and strategies, you are well on your way to becoming a successful Uber driver in the ever-evolving sharing economy.

Chapter 5. Decoding TaskRabbit: Making the Most from Tasks

TaskRabbit, founder Leah Busque's brainchild, has surfaced as a remarkable platform in the arena of the sharing economy. It functions as an online and mobile marketplace that matches freelance labor with local demand, connecting people who need tasks done with "Taskers" ready to perform them. With services ranging from simple chores like grocery shopping to more complex jobs like minor home renovations, TaskRabbit has molded a micro-employment landscape in over 50 cities in the United States, Canada, and the United Kingdom. Let's dive deeper into understanding how TaskRabbit operates and how you can make the most out of it as a "Tasker".

5.1. Understanding the TaskRabbit Model

The first thing to understand is how TaskRabbit's business model functions. Once you sign up as a "Tasker", you'll be able to view and choose tasks that suit your skills, schedule, and rate. Prospective clients outline the task they need completing, their location, and a proposed fee. As a Tasker, you can make a counteroffer, and the client decides who they prefer for the task based on ratings, skills, and price.

Unlike ride-sharing or room-renting platforms, TaskRabbit focuses more on a range of services, like handiwork, delivery tasks, and cleaning, among others. By capitalizing on a broad category of tasks, TaskRabbit henceforth offers a bigger potential for earnings in various niches.

5.2. Setting Up Your Tasker Profile

Creating a rock-solid profile is crucial in your TaskRabbit journey. Displaying your skills and expertise prominently can significantly impact your potential earnings. Make sure to follow these pointers:

- Mention your skills: List out all your skills, even if they seem mundane. Be it fixing a leak, assembling furniture, running errands, or professional skills like graphic designing or writing, add them all to your repertoire. The wider the skill set, the more tasks you can take up.

- Be specific: Under each skill, be precise about your expertise. For instance, if you are adept at assembling IKEA furniture, list specific models that you've worked on.

- Responsive rate: A critical factor that the clients review while picking a Tasker is their responsive rate. A high response rate implies that you are serious and professional about taking up tasks.

5.3. Pricing Wisely

Pricing your services correctly can either make or break your venture into TaskRabbit. Too high a price might discourage clients, while a fee too low might not be worth your effort. To determine a competitive price point:

- Evaluate the market: Check out what other Taskers with similar skills are charging for comparison. This will give you a reasonable idea of the prevalent rates.

- Consider the time commitment: Account for how much time it takes to complete a task when calculating your rates. This includes not only the time dedicated to performing the task but also the travel time.

5.4. Cultivating Client Relationships

Building a strong relationship with your clients can help secure repeat business. Here are some strategies to ensure happy clients:

- Communicate effectively: Always clarify any doubts regarding task details before you start. Keep clients informed about your progress.

- Consistent Quality: Ensure the quality of your work prolongs consistently. Scaling up does not mean scaling down on the quality that you deliver.

Thinking outside of the task box and understanding the diverse avenues of services that TaskRabbit offers can work wonders towards maximizing your income potential. Tune in to what the market demands and mould your skills to fit these needs. With the right skillset, competitive pricing, a quick response rate, and a commitment to quality, you are now perfectly poised to make the most of this exciting platform. Don't forget - TaskRabbit, much like any other platform, is what you make of it. Lay a solid foundation, work persistently and before you know it, you'll be thriving in this dynamic, sharing economy.

Chapter 6. Leveraging Lyft for Lucrative Gains

Let's begin by demystifying the rideshare company that has been making waves in the sharing economy - Lyft. With its unique pink emblem and a firm commitment to building better communities, Lyft has proven to be a golden opportunity for individuals to make money while offering a valuable service to their community.

6.1. Understanding the Lyft Ecosystem

Lyft operates on a simple business model—offering on-demand ride services for customers through a mobile app. Every transaction is handled digitally, from ride orders and cancellations, to payments and ratings. As a Lyft driver, you're not an employee of the company, you're an independent contractor, using your own car to provide rides. This approach gives you considerably more flexibility than traditional jobs and that's one of the many alluring factors of driving for Lyft.

6.2. Becoming a Lyft Driver

To start with, you need to meet Lyft's requirements and guidelines to become one of their drivers. The basic prerequisites include being at least 21 years old, owning a 4-door vehicle in good condition, and carrying a valid U.S. driver's license. Additionally, you will also need to pass a background check, have personal auto insurance, and meet specific state and city guidelines. Once registered and approved, you're all set to start taking ride requests.

6.3. Capitalize on Peak Times and Locations

There's a surefire strategy to maximize profits when driving for Lyft - it's picking up rides during peak hours. Peak hours usually revolve around early mornings (when people are going to work or airport), late evenings (when people are returning from work), and later in the night during weekends, where riders are either going to party spots or coming back from them.

Similarly, driving in busy locations such as downtown areas, business districts, airports, or places with nightlife increases your chances of getting more ride requests. Being strategic about when and where you drive can significantly increase your earning potential.

6.4. Importance of High Customer Ratings

Lyft drivers are rated by their customers. A high rating works in favor of drivers as it increases their credibility and hence, more passengers are likely to choose them. So, it's essential you provide excellent service to ensure high ratings. Keeping your car clean, being polite, offering amenities like water or phone chargers, and ensuring a safe and smooth ride can go a long way in getting positive ratings.

Additionally, it's worth noting that consistently low ratings can put your status as a Lyft driver at risk. Therefore, providing stellar service should always be a top priority.

6.5. Maximizing Profit with Lyft's Incentives and Bonuses

To make driving for Lyft more lucrative, the company provides various incentives and bonuses. There's the 'Weekly Ride Challenge', where if you complete a certain number of rides in a week, you get an extra bonus. This not only provides an immediate cash incentive but also pushes drivers to be more active in their hours of operation.

Additionally, Lyft also offers a 'Power Driver Bonus' for drivers who complete a certain number of rides during peak hours. The percent added to your earnings depends on your location and the total number of rides completed. Planning your schedule to meet these challenges can significantly boost your earnings.

6.6. Tips and Tolls: Extra Income

One overlooked aspect with ride-share earnings is the potential revenue from tips and tolls. Lyft allows passengers to tip drivers digitally through the app, and all of this goes directly to the driver. Delivering a comfortable, efficient, and friendly ride often encourages riders to tip.

Moreover, the expenses of tolls are compensated for by Lyft. So, when you pass through a toll, the cost is added to the passenger's fare and you receive the amount as part of your earnings.

6.7. The Lyft Express Drive Program

If you don't own a vehicle or if your current car doesn't meet the Lyft's vehicle requirements, the 'Lyft Express Drive program' is a viable alternative. It allows you to rent a car to use for Lyft driving. The rental costs can be offset based on the number of rides provided per week, which means as you drive more, you can take home a larger profit.

Driving for Lyft is not just about delivering people to their destinations; it's also about delivering exceptional service, being strategic in your approach, and maximizing the opportunities provided. With ample motivation and the right strategies, leveraging Lyft for lucrative gains becomes a significant and viable earning opportunity in the sharing economy.

Chapter 7. Postmates Profits: How to Cash In On Your Free Time

Today's gig economy presents an exciting opportunity to generate extra income in your spare time. One such venture is Postmates— a delivery service that is active in hundreds of cities worldwide. In this chapter, we will walk you through proven strategies for maximizing your profits on Postmates.

7.1. Getting Started with Postmates

In its origins, Postmates was a delivery company focused on transporting goods from businesses to consumers. However, over time it evolved into a much-loved food delivery service allowing anyone to get anything from anywhere delivered on-demand.

To become a Postmates delivery driver - also referred to as a Postmate - you need to be at least 18 years old, own a smartphone for the Postmates Fleet app (the driver's app), and have access to a vehicle (or bicycle, in select markets). You also need to pass a background check that evaluates your driving record and criminal history.

7.2. Understanding the Financial Model

Postmates' payment model is relatively straightforward. It's made up of:

- A rate per picked-up order

- A rate per dropped-off order

- A per minute-waited rate for any time spent at the pickup location

- A per-mile rate for the distance between the pickup & drop-off location

Plus, you keep all tips received. Each city has different rates, and you can always find this information in the Postmates Fleet app.

7.3. Maximizing Your Earnings

Becoming a Postmate is a gratifying way to earn extra income. However, it becomes even more lucrative when you incorporate strategies designed to maximize your earnings. Here are some tips:

1. Optimize your Schedule: Target the busiest times—generally lunch (11am-2pm) and dinner (5pm-9pm) hours. Also, weekends typically have a higher demand.

2. Accept Multiple Orders: The Postmates Fleet app has a multi-order feature which allows you to stack orders, meaning you can pick up and drop off multiple orders at a time. This increases your earning potential.

3. Choose the Right Vehicle: Vehicles with good gas mileage are best for urban areas with heavy traffic. For areas with short distances and heavy traffic, bicycles save on gas and maintenance costs.

4. Smart Acceptance: Be selective with the orders you accept. Orders from high-end restaurants and gourmet grocery stores usually involve larger transactions and higher tip potential.

7.4. Navigating the Challenges

Just like any job, working as a Postmate has its challenges:

1. Parking: In congested city areas, finding quick and legal parking can be challenging. Get familiar with areas you service often and note the best parking spots.

2. Wear and Tear: Your vehicle will accrue mileage. Regular maintenance is essential, and costs should be factored into your earnings.

3. Safety: This applies to both road safety and ensuring that you're comfortable with the delivery location. If a delivery location appears unsafe, contact Postmates support.

4. Taxes: Remember, you'll need to pay taxes on your earnings as an independent contractor. Keep track of your income and expenses throughout the year.

7.5. Customer Service is Key

A significant part of a Postmate's income comes from tips. Exceptional service can often lead to better tips. Always be professional, prompt, and communicate with your customers if issues arise that could delay delivery.

7.6. Expand Your Opportunities

Think of your job as a Postmate as the initial step in exploring the gig economy. Once you've successfully plunged into this venture, consider exploring various income streams such as Uber, Lyft, or Airbnb to maximize your profitability.

Being a delivery driver (Postmate) is an attractive prospect in the evolving gig economy. It offers both freedom and flexibility, with the potential for sound economic returns. By optimizing your scheduling, providing excellent customer service, and wisely choosing delivery orders, you can certainly unlock a lucrative stream of additional income. Pioneering into this dynamic field, you're not just earning—you are also shaping the future of work and economy. Start your journey with Postmates and explore the untapped potential of the gig economy today.

Chapter 8. Broadening Horizons with Turo and Getaround

As the sharing economy continues to reign supreme in the modern world, it is important to also focus on other up and coming platforms that have started to prove their weight in gold. Two such platforms are Turo and Getaround — car sharing services that allow you to put your idle vehicle to work and potentially generate substantial income. With their peer-to-peer car sharing model, an individual's vehicle becomes an asset capable of creating income as opposed to being just another expense. Let's dive in and get a comprehensive understanding of these platforms and how you can profit from them.

8.1. Turning idle assets into income streams with Turo

Turo is not your typical car rental service. It allows car owners to list their vehicles on its platform, and drivers then rent these vehicles. The business model Turo uses, often compared to Airbnb, has disrupted the traditional car rental industry in similar fashion.

To start making money on Turo, begin by listing your car. It's free and can be done on turo.com or the Turo app. You'll need to provide in-depth descriptions and upload high-quality photos of your vehicle. The more information you provide, the more confident renters will be when choosing your car.

You have full control over your vehicle — you set the price, availability, and the rules. It is important to set a competitive price, but if you're not sure what to charge, Turo provides a tool that suggests a price based on market value, location, time of year, and other data.

When a renter chooses your vehicle, you coordinate with them where to pick up the vehicle. You also have the choice to deliver or not. It is essential that you have your vehicle clean and in excellent condition, ready for the renter. Turo has a backup plan for owners with a protection package that includes $1 million in liability insurance and varying levels of contract protection for your vehicle.

8.2. Broadening your revenue stream with Getaround

Getaround is another popular car sharing platform that allows you to rent out your car when it's not in use. Like Turo, Getaround offers $1 million in insurance coverage, roadside assistance, and 24/7 support for listed cars.

Listing your car on Getaround is free; the platform only takes its share when you start making money. Getaround car owners set their rental prices and also the times their cars are available for rent.

A unique feature of Getaround is their patented Getaround Connect® technology. This device allows renters to locate and unlock your vehicle from their phone, meaning you don't need to physically meet renters. This approach makes renting more flexible and means you can earn money without extensive time investment.

8.3. Maximizing revenue from car sharing platforms

Both Turo and Getaround offer innovative ways to turn your idle car into an income generator. However, there are strategies that you can follow to enhance the income you generate from these platforms.

Optimize vehicle availability: Renters need cars at all different times, so aim to align your car's availability with peak demand times.

Maintain your vehicle: Regular servicing and cleaning can often equate to more rentals, as users tend to pick vehicles that look good and are reliable.

Provide a unique experience: Do you have a unique or desirable car? Special vehicles, like a vintage Porsche or a brand-new Tesla, can command more money on Turo and Getaround.

Navigate peak seasons: Holiday seasons and weekends are often peak times for car rentals. Consider adjusting rates during these peak periods to maximize profits.

8.4. The drawbacks and potential risks

While the allure of easy money is tempting, it's worth considering the potential risks and drawbacks of listing your vehicle on car sharing platforms. Some of these include:

Wear and tear: Additional driving can speed up the wear of your car and may lead to more regular maintenance or repairs.

Unpredictable renters: Despite background checks by Turo and Getaround, there's always a risk that renters may not treat your vehicle well.

Insurance complications: While both platforms provide liability insurance, there might be gaps that may not protect you against all scenarios. It's essential to fully understand the coverage parameters.

Car sharing platforms like Turo and Getaround offer an excellent way to put your idle car to work by turning it into an asset that generates income. If you're comfortable with the risks and are willing to invest time in listing and managing your vehicle, these platforms could provide a significant boost to your income in the dynamic sharing economy.

Chapter 9. Setting Prices and Maximizing Profits

Understanding the intricacies of pricing can be the difference between success and mediocrity in the sharing economy. Profit margins are crucial; they can determine whether your venture into this new economy is worthwhile. Thus, first on your agenda is to master the art of setting prices and maximizing profits.

9.1. Calculating Costs

Before you set any prices, you should first have an understanding of your costs. Both Airbnb and Uber allow you to operate your business directly from your home or personal car, representing a fabulous chance to convert otherwise fixed personal expenses into revenue-generating assets.

On Airbnb, costs to consider include mortgage or rent, utility bills, the cost of cleaning and maintaining the space, insurance, and any necessary licenses or permits. On Uber, costs comprise car payments, insurance, maintenance, depreciation, gas, and occasionally tolls. Subtracting these costs from your total revenue will give you an idea of your potential profit. Being aware of these costs will allow you to set realistic rates for your services.

9.2. Analyzing the Market

Market analysis is critical when setting your prices. This involves looking at similar listings or rides and seeing what others are charging. For example, if you're renting out a room on Airbnb, look at what others with similar rooms in your area are charging. Additionally, consider factors such as seasonality and special events. Also, it's vital to keep track of your competitors' offerings—additional amenities, better locations, and outstanding reviews can justify a higher price, and you must adjust your offerings accordingly.

Similarly, for Uber, understand the rate the company suggests but also monitor surge pricing times. Surge prices kick in during high demand periods, so aligning your driving times with these periods can greatly enhance your earnings.

9.3. Dynamic Pricing

Dynamic pricing is a powerful tool in your arsenal. This pricing strategy allows you to change prices based on demands in the market. With Airbnb, you can adjust your prices depending on the season, day of the week, and surrounding events.

On Uber, while you cannot directly control the fare, you can make use of surge pricing periods and choose to offer your services only during busy times, thus effectively deploying dynamic pricing for your benefit.

9.4. Understanding the Value You Provide

In the sharing economy, you must understand the value you provide to your customers. Successful hosts and drivers know that value is not necessarily about low prices.

For Airbnb hosts, value can be clean and comfortable accommodations, a distinctive and inviting space, additional amenities, or excellent customer service. For Uber drivers, value can mean a pristine and comfortable vehicle, conscientious driving, or exceptional customer service, such as offering water, phone chargers, or even local tips and recommendations. Understanding this will allow you to price your service appropriately without undervaluing what you offer.

9.5. Experiment and Adjust

Finally, do not be afraid to experiment with your pricing and then adjust it based on the results you achieve. Pricing is an ongoing process and you need to be responsive to changes in the market, feedback from customers, and your personal income needs. If you don't see the bookings you want on Airbnb, test lowering your prices for a while to see if demand increases. With Uber, keep track of when and where you make most of your money and adapt your driving schedule accordingly.

In conclusion, setting prices and maximizing profits in the sharing economy is a blend of understanding your costs, knowing the market, adjusting prices according to demand, understanding the value you provide to your customers, and always being willing to experiment and adjust as needed to maximize your profits. The combination of these is the approach that will likely yield the best financial outcome in your new venture. Remember, your involvement in the sharing economy is not just to make ends meet but to use your resources in the most efficient way possible, providing you the opportunity to flourish in this new economy model.

Chapter 10. Building a Stellar Reputation in the Sharing Economy

In the sharing economy, reputation is more than just a reflection of your character—it's a tangible asset that could determine the success of your venture. It is critical to build a trustworthy and reliable image since it influences how others interact with, rent from, or employ you. This understanding can pave your way to a robust, thriving business within the sharing economy.

10.1. Understanding the Significance of Reputation

Reputation is the cornerstone of the sharing economy. Platforms like Airbnb, Uber, and Etsy are built on trust, and this trust stems from the collective feedback and ratings users leave behind. This feedback system contributes to a digital reputation that plays a significant role in shaping future interactions. An Airbnb host with a low rating may struggle to attract bookings, while an Uber driver with rave reviews can enjoy consistent business.

Building a strong reputation can lead to more business transactions, increase profitability, and contribute to the overall growth of your venture. On the flip side, a poor reputation could repel potential customers, diminishing your growth potential. Essentially, maintaining a stellar reputation is integral to thriving in the sharing economy.

10.2. Reputation Management Strategies

Improving your reputation within the sharing economy isn't merely about preventing negative reviews—it's about consistently delivering excellent service that compels users to leave positive feedback.

1. Quality Service: The key to building a great reputation on these platforms is to provide exceptional service. Ensure your offerings are clean, well-maintained, and as advertised. Strive to exceed customer expectations.

2. Clear Communication: Establish open lines of communication with your customers. Respond promptly to queries and be clear about what you offer and what can be expected.

3. Honesty and Transparency: Truthfulness is valued in the sharing economy. Honesty about the products or services offered, pricing, and policies helps build trust with customers.

4. Handle Complaints Effectively: How you manage complaints can directly impact your online reputation. Attempt to resolve issues promptly and adequately. Always remain professional, polite, and understanding.

5. Request for Reviews: Encourage satisfied customers to leave reviews detailing their positive experiences. However, never coerce or offer incentives for reviews; this can lead to a violation of platform rules or be seen as dishonest.

10.3. Leveraging Reviews and Feedback

In the sharing economy, feedback is the lifeblood of your reputation. A string of positive reviews can transform a humble Airbnb listing into a sought-after destination.

- Prompt Response: Always thank your customers for their feedback. It not only shows appreciation but also signals that you're attentive and open to suggestions, which can result in more positive reviews in the future.

- Critical Feedback: Negative reviews may tarnish your reputation temporarily, but they also offer valuable insights into areas that need improvement. Learn to use negative feedback productively. Fix the issues pointed out—if the complaints are valid—and move forward.

- Feature Positive Reviews: Showcase your positive reviews to enhance trust and entice new customers. However, remember to obtain the reviewer's permission before posting their feedback elsewhere.

10.4. Building Trust with Customers

Trust plays a fundamental role in the sharing economy. Because transactions happen between strangers, the onus is on you as a service provider to create an environment of trust.

- Be Consistent: Consistency in delivering high-quality services can help you build credibility and robust differentiating identity. Over time, this consistency can cement your reputation as a trustworthy, reliable choice in the market.

- Be Professional: Maintaining professionalism goes a long way in establishing trust. This includes prompt communication, courteous behavior, and honoring commitments.

- Value Privacy: Respecting your customers' privacy generates trust. Be clear about which information you'll need for the transaction to proceed and safeguard the data diligently.

- Invest in Safety Measures: Especially relevant for platforms like Airbnb and Uber, demonstrating proactive measures for customer safety can boost customer confidence and directly influence your reputation.

By incorporating these strategies, you can start building a stellar reputation in the sharing economy. Remember, each positive interaction, each five-star review, and each satisfied customer contributes to a reputation that can set you apart in this competitive space. Build it carefully, treat it as a precious resource, and it will serve as the bedrock of your success in the sharing economy.

Chapter 11. Legal Aspects and Tax Considerations in the Sharing Economy

It's no secret that the sharing economy can pave the way to meaningful income. However, it's not just about leveraging existing assets and putting in hard work. One must navigate a labyrinth of legalities, requirements, and stipulations to fully capitalize on these opportunities and avoid potential pitfalls. This chapter is dedicated to enlightening you about the legal implications and tax considerations integral to platforms like Airbnb, Uber, and similar platforms.

11.1. Legal Frameworks: Understanding and Adhering to the Rules

Before you begin your journey in the sharing economy, it's essential to understand the legal frameworks involved. Each country, state, and even municipality has different rules regulating different sharing platforms, and it's incumbent upon you to adhere to these stipulations.

Airbnb, for starters, provides a set of recommended guidelines. However, these should be treated as starting points, not exhaustive rules. The actual regulations you need to comply with can be complex depending upon your location. For example, some cities may require you to acquire a license or permit before listing your property. Moreover, there could be restrictions on the total number of days you can rent out your place in a year.

It's similar with Uber and other ride-sharing apps too. Different jurisdictions mandate different requirements—be it a special license, insurance, or specific checks on the vehicle and driver. Ignoring these requirements can result in fines, litigation, or even the prohibition from operating completely.

Keep yourself updated about the regulations in your area by visiting the official websites of the local government, getting email updates, attending meetings or seminars, or hiring an attorney who specializes in sharing economy laws.

11.2. Insurance Considerations: Necessary Coverages

Insurance is another crucial legal aspect that you need to consider. While companies like Uber and Airbnb provide some insurance, these may not be enough to cover all potential scenarios or damages. Insurance policies are legally binding contracts and understanding their subtext is critical before signing up.

With Airbnb, for instance, the host protection insurance program covers up to $1 million in damages for third-party liability claims. However, it doesn't cover personal injury or property damages caused by various scenarios like natural calamities, intentional acts, or loss of earnings. Separate homeowners or renters insurance may be needed to supplement these gaps.

Uber provides drivers with an insurance coverage that varies depending on the ride phase - whether the driver is waiting for a request, en-route to pick up a rider, or dropping them off. Again, gaps persist and these may need to be filled with additional personal auto insurance.

11.3. Zoning and Homeowner Association Regulations

Next, one must also understand Zoning and Homeowner Association (HOA) regulations. These rules, usually governed at the municipal level or by a board of residents, define what activities can be performed in certain areas or properties.

Many cities restrict commercial activities in residential zones—which may include short-term rentals like Airbnb. Violations can result in fines or even litigation. Similar restrictions may also exist in HOA rules. Before starting your sharing economy venture, it's important to research and comply with these rules.

11.4. Contractual Obligations: Tenancy and Subletting Issues

If you are a tenant yourself, you need to bear in mind your rental contract and its terms. Subletting your rented property may be prohibited unless explicitly agreed upon by your landlord. Violation of these terms can lead to eviction or legal trouble.

Similarly, Uber drivers must ensure they have permission from the title owner if they do not own the car themselves.

11.5. Understanding Tax Implications in the Sharing Economy

The sharing economy's financial rewards are tied up in tax requirements. Regardless of the platform you choose, the income you earn should be declared on your tax returns, and appropriate amounts should be paid.

Airbnb hosts, for instance, are typically seen as running a rental property business by the IRS in the United States. This means you must report your income and expenses on Schedule E of your tax return. However, if you are renting for only short periods (14 days or less in a year), you may not have to pay tax on that income under the Masters exception rule.

Uber drivers must file a Schedule C with their tax returns, as they are considered independent contractors. All the income, along with the expenses incurred (like gas, maintenance, insurance), should be reported.

Additionally, sales tax, lodging tax, or VAT may apply depending on your area of operation. Services like Airbnb and Uber generally handle VAT and sales tax collection and remittance; however, for lodging tax, hosts may have to collect and remit themselves.

Make sure to carve out a chunk of your earnings to cover tax obligations. Consult with a tax advisor, particularly one experienced with sharing economy taxes, to ensure you are correctly reporting income and claiming all legal deductions and credits.

11.6. Wrapping Up

Entering the sharing economy is an exciting venture, but it demands a comprehensive understanding of the legal and tax implications. Adhering to the rules not only helps you avoid penalties but also paves the way for a successful and sustainable business.

Remember, this chapter is a guideline and not a substitute for professional legal or tax advice. Always consult with legal and tax professionals when you're in doubt or need further clarification. After all, ensuring you're on the right side of the law is as crucial as your business plan, if not more. Happy sharing!